from the earthen drum of my body

Deborah Ramos

BLUE LIGHT PRESS ◆ 1ST WORLD PUBLISHING

SAN FRANCISCO ◆ FAIRFIELD ◆ DELHI

from the earthen drum of my body
Copyright ©2018 by Deborah Ramos

All rights reserved. Printed in the United States of America. No part of this book may be used or reproduced in any manner whatsoever without written permission except in the case of brief quotations embodied in critical articles and reviews. For information contact:

1st World Library
PO Box 2211
Fairfield, IA 52556
www.1stworldpublishing.com

Blue Light Press
www.bluelightpress.com
Email: bluelightpress@aol.com

Book & Cover Design
Melanie Gendron
melaniegendron999@gmail.com

Cover Art
"Rising Goddess" by Deborah Ramos

Interior Art
Deborah Ramos

Author Photo
June Price

First Edition

ISBN: 978-1-4218-3801-4

A word on poetry

Give me unexpected clarity.
Give me subtle cohesiveness.
Give me poetry that brings life
to the otherwise mundane and unnoticed.
Make me pay attention
to the words scribbled in the margins.

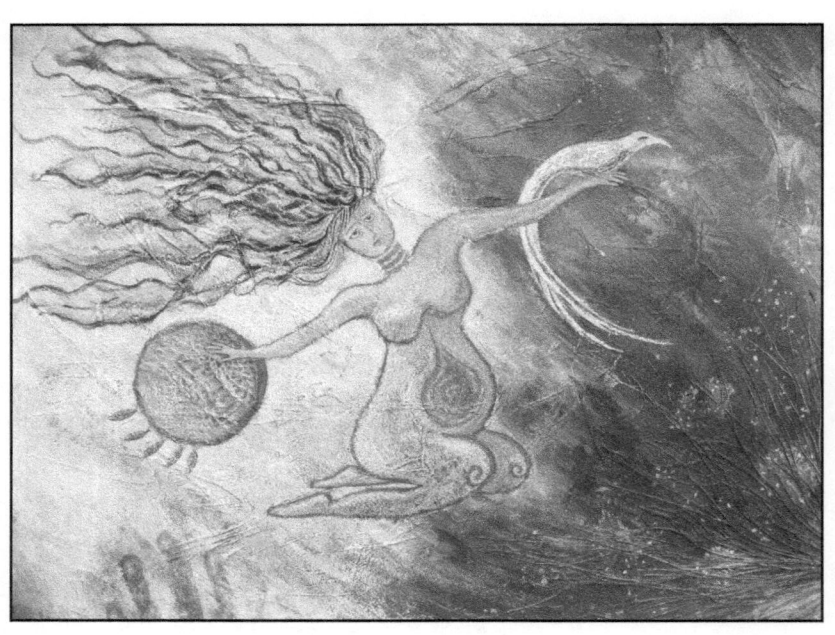

This book is dedicated to
my Mongolian Warrior,
my dream-catcher.
You touched my pomegranate center
and released the wild woman.

Acknowledgements

I love the power of words splashed across the canvas
screaming purples and turquoise.
The persistence of dreaming, the sacred walk,
and knowing what you're longing for.

Poems previously published:

"Sunset Silhouette," *San Diego Poetry Annual, 2010*

"Thread Bare," *WTF! Spring 2011, Rattlesnake Press*

"Winter's Eclipse," *A Year in Ink Anthology 2014, SD Writer's Ink*

"Just Another Lobster Poem," *River of Earth and Sky: Poems for the Twenty-First Century*

"When Columbus Never Actually Landed in America," *A Year in Ink Anthology 2016, SD Writer's Ink*

The following poems
are part of a collection that won the
Best Unpublished Poetry Chapbook 2010 category,
awarded by the San Diego Book Awards Association:

Just Another Lobster Poem
Night Bed
Hungry River
Sunset Silhouette
Road Warriors

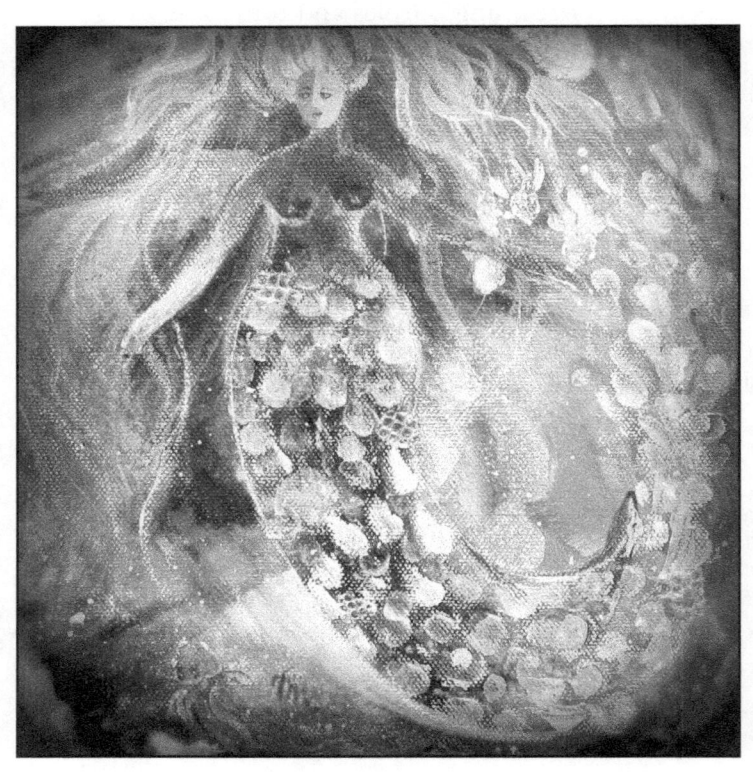

Table of Contents

Just Another Lobster Poem 1
night bed 2
Just deep enough 3
Volcanic Reef 5
divine nourishment 7
Thread Bare 8
Jeweled Codpiece 9
Winter's Eclipse 11
Love, everlasting 12
My House is the Sky 14
Heart of the Canyon 17
Rock Bottom 18
Reckless Seduction 20
Sunset Silhouette 21
Couples Counseling 23
Abandoned Tribes 24
Road Warriors 26
Shaman's Toolbox 29
Interview With Coyote 30
Beneath the Canopy 32
When Columbus Never Actually Landed in America 34
When I am Poetry 36
About the Author 37

Just Another Lobster Poem

Vagina dentata,
hungry and hidden
buried deep inside
come hither
glistening folds.

Beware.
Grizzly Woman
crawls out of her fur
to devour mischievous
out-thrusting manhood
with ferocious fangs.

Freud said it's the
male subconscious fear
of castration by
She Who Already Broke Hers Off.

Revenge,
a penis made of stone.
Teeth shatter and
She-bear returns
to the womb of her cave.

night bed

come close,
let me splatter you
with my primal perfume.

bodies fuse together.
the taste soaks into
your dripping chocolate skin.

our echoes arouse
the sleeping meadow,
stir the steady pines.
ears perk from their night beds.

clouds roll across the moon.
sticky embraces smolder
into dreaming.

Just deep enough . . .

Watery fingers of seaweed
wind around my ankles,
creep up to my knees
push against my thighs.

I resist the pull to deeper worlds.
I only want to be close to you,
to skim the surface of your wanting foam.

Let me slide in and out of tide pools,
inhale the tang of the salty air
and moisten my skin with your spray.

I leave with the moon
and return with receding sand.

Volcanic Reef

Sea glass eyes buried
in ancient grains of urchins and corals.

Remnants of seaweed feet
trace skeletons of volcanic shells.

Thousand year old winds
hail the Mermaid Queen,
secretly stolen by the reckless tide.

divine nourishment

bathed in crimson,
i sit facing the east.
my third eye opens.
silent waves of dawn
rinse the sinewy chasm
of my beginnings,
my endings,
and all that has been.

soaked in golden smoke,
ancient hide stretches wet,
shrinks tight around a hoop of fire.
the rhythmic pulse
circles our naked alter.
sacred honey-ripe vulva
drums you from the Elk-cave.

serpentine bodies press close.
primal desires ignite smoldering walls.
the canal fills,
and my river becomes yours.

Thread Bare

Flame-retardant silhouettes
finger up weeping walls,
candles glaring cat eyes.

Another story burns into buttery flesh,
your name seared onto my breast.
Scars camouflaged in secret.

Plum nipples, firm from your touch,
unaware of the inky assault.

Should our love letters fade to thread-bare silk,
a bleeding gash will rip and pour,
just to change the spelling of you.

Jeweled Codpiece

Heliodor ribbons stretch across
the downy mattress,
hand-stitched with opal silk,
cool and slippery to the touch.
Shadow feet tip-toe
down nightly stairs.

Misty moonstone bodies
richly adorn the peeling tabletop.
Clay bowl of plums and pears
spill ripe to feed swelling succulence.

Polished in black pearls of sweat,
the pilgrimage hurricanes,
sipping silver flasks of fresh wine.
Carnelian walls pillow screaming bites.

Ponds of ancient tiger's eye adobe
press into burnished satin skin.
The infallible feast of flesh and sapphire
dims and our fluted
song falls silent.

Winter's Eclipse

Twilight trails stain muddy hooves,
pounding beneath lunar smoke.

A labyrinth of flesh and fluid
waits for the eclipse
to find the edges,
the dim perimeter
of her wanting.

Antlers high, cimmerian man-elk
ruts to the cool moon center.

Velvet-rich bone, aged virility,
takes her
guards her,
keeps her painfully near.

Love, everlasting

She begs him to save her,
thin with hope, hands knotted,
hair twisted into ropes of silver.
She summons him closer,
to sneak past the reptilian tail
that spirals the castle keep.

Pearly scales and ivory claws
line the damp stairway.
Weeping, she vanishes to her chamber
to avoid the icy stare of her beastly guardian.

Banished from the abyss of fire,
the basilisk is burdened for eternity
to guard his delicate treasure.
Metallic scales have turned to granite.
Jeweled wings melt into walls.
With crimson eyes fixed upon her,
the mighty serpent king
has become the fortified tower.

Beaten by the decades,
her dark warrior returns
to pierce the draconian heart
and reclaim his divine angel.
The ghostly citadel stands before him,
vines rooted to walls, filling cracks
the way dawn fills shadows.

Armed with bone and steel,
the willing hero circles
the fusion of reptile and stone,
and makes the ascent.
Smoke fills his lungs;
leathery walls breathe at his back.

Startled, the beast betrays his prisoner
and casts his gaze toward the intruder.
The fatal glance ends the assault,
and the deadly silence lifts.

Cloaked in faded silk, she finds her lover,
heart barely beating beneath his marbled skin,
frozen in perpetual rescue.
She coils around her statue warrior,
welcomes him sweetly,
the flesh of her heart pressed
against the cold stone of his,
eternally embraced.

My House is the Sky

Mistress of the Wild Beasts
hunts quail near the fertile banks of the Nile.
Floodwaters give birth to you every morning.

Cycles of the Dark Maiden
separated you from your king
and tangled him
in the roots of the Huluppu Tree.

He once worshipped your amber feet,
tended the melting cone of myrrh
that scents the raven of your hair.
He painted papyrus with visions
of spitting cobras to honor his queen.

Your ritual weeping hailed me.
Burning incense summoned me.
Ripened honey wine intoxicated me.
I, the Dancing Moon Priestess,
bells on my ankles,
jeweled fingertips,
entered the Divine Temple.

The pulse of my drum
pulled your phallic lord
through vines of rippling water.
The song of your twisted harp
 promised him eternal life
at the mouth of the frothing sea.

Incarnated life to life, fire to fire,
you will remember me,
Lotus Sister from All Dreams Before,
lighting your way to the Womb Mother,
where Hathor arches over the earth
to reclaim her Crocodile King.

Heart of the Canyon

Vanishing moons circle the mesa.
Wild rose sweetens the parched canyon.

As the saffron morning rises, a woven bed opens
to invoke the dreaming dawn.

Sun-drenched adobe walls shade
graffiti gods etched into sandstone.

Yucca sandals pad along a windswept trail.
Twisted junipers brush against sweat soaked skin.

Honey gold maidens dance in the central plaza,
cleansed in songs made of corn and pollen.

Raven's red stones heat cooking baskets.
Hot coals roast piñon nuts and figs.

Deep in the kiva womb, Kachina spirits tell stories.
Ancestors emerge from the smoke-blackened edge of creation.

Sudden winds push rumbling clouds from the oceanic sky,
leaving the cliff palace empty and scorched.

The Children of Summer
abandon the dry, ochre earth
to follow the fertile trail of the serpent river
and rebuild the stained layers of ancient seas.

Rock Bottom

First time I hit rock bottom,
I thought I was alone.
Glo-stick bracelets cracked around my wrist
lit the way like a coal miners hat.
Seems to be a lot of us
down here sharing this rock.

Puma said she hit rock bottom, too,
so we did a healing.
Arms and beating hearts
wrapped around her,
chanting womyn's songs.
She walked through tunnels of angels.
Voices sang her in and out of flutes

I taught Puma how to dance with bats,
how to wing through shadows,
how to keep secrets.

Remember Stellaluna, I said.
When that baby bat hit rock bottom,
she landed in a nest
and swiftly became more bird than bat.
She slept with the moon.
She perched on tree limbs,
eating bugs with her bird brothers.
Mother bird wasn't happy when she
found her 3 babies and a bat
hanging upside down
from her woven ribbon basket.
She flapped her mad wings
and chased Stellaluna away.

Some light their way out with glo-stick bracelets.
Some bounce through the dark.
Puma unraveled to her wick
until she caught on fire.
Rising lava lifted her
to the earth's blossoming rim,
where the sun's trail was fresh and new.

Reckless Seduction

I sauntered in with a wine buzz,
tight jeans, and a pink angora sweater.
A California girl perched on a bar stool
in a dim corner of Seattle.

A shot of tequila and tabasco
burned my throat
with the promise of intoxication.

The air, heavy with smoke
vibrated with retro rock and roll.

I flirted with freedom and begged
dark edges to become my refuge.

But she found me,
despite my attempts
to escape her callous winter.

Hands reaching deep in my back pockets,
she pulled me away from
the cowboy with sad eyes,
his stories spilling on the scuffed floor.

She spelled my name in the
steam of whiskey breath
and surrendered her hardened heart.

Seduced again by the
familiar dance of forgiveness,
the final sweep of mercy across the floor,
my soul cocooned by the
hurricane of this moonless night

Sunset Silhouette

Patent leather pumps,
two sizes too big, scuffed patches of glossy yellow,
crookedly clomp along the boardwalk.
Too many roads, too many miles.

Purple paisley skirt,
faded as a smudge,
sways through the crowd.
Too short to flatter the
varicose veins spidering thin legs.
Too many lifetimes, too long ago.

Colorless linen blouse
flutters like a loose sail.
Too thin to hide the protruding clavicles.
Too little food and too many slams
in the shadows.

Malnourished sunken face,
hides beneath layers of cakey make-up.
Too many cigarettes and too many hours
soliciting in the salty sun.

Pomegranate hair,
brittle and broken, commands
the crumbling architecture of humanity.
Curved shoulders and hips
weathered into bony angles.

Leaning on the seawall,
she blows a smoke ring
and winks a crinkled eye

at her imaginary lover
beneath the black stone
of the falling night.

Couples Counseling

She was only seeking salvation
when they joined hands and
spoke to the social worker.
There is a brighter side of
living in the street.

She zipped up her sleeping bag
and thought she'd lost weight.
Sidewalk vagabonds press into corners,
one bicycle, a backpack and their disability checks.
A two-income family now.

A tent pitched in the park
thinly shelters the couple while they
watch the Sea World fireworks.
If there ever was a true sign from God,
that's it.

Abandoned Tribes

We call ours Coalition for the Homeless.
Transients enjoy dinner, a Clint Eastwood movie,
and leave with scarves, socks, and loaves of bread.
They call theirs Famine Relief Centers.
Refugees get de-wormed,
rations for the 2-week walk back home
and seeds for planting.

Posted on her sedulous blog,
the plump bleached lady complains.
Too many applications to fill out,
too many phone calls to return,
and fuel assistance is a bureaucratic nightmare.
But her fluffy bleached-children win
scholarships to summer camp.
It's a full time job being poor.

A black satin sleep mask
keeps her circadian clock in check
as the western world folds into foreclosure.
Send the kids to boarding school
and check into a homeless shelter
until the Affordable Housing application is approved.

If only those hungry Ethiopians had the internet,
they might learn something about being poor.

Street remnants bear forgotten scars,
childhood pox bubble into septic sores
beneath emaciated rags.
Clusters of flies dance in eye sockets
to black out sizzling shards of light.
Natures sleeping mask.
Rejoice, it's summer camp all year round.

Ghostly orphans pile into sewer pipes
like a tribe of abandoned puppies,
nudging for an empty, withering teat,
as the night weeps a sad note
on a one-stringed African violin.

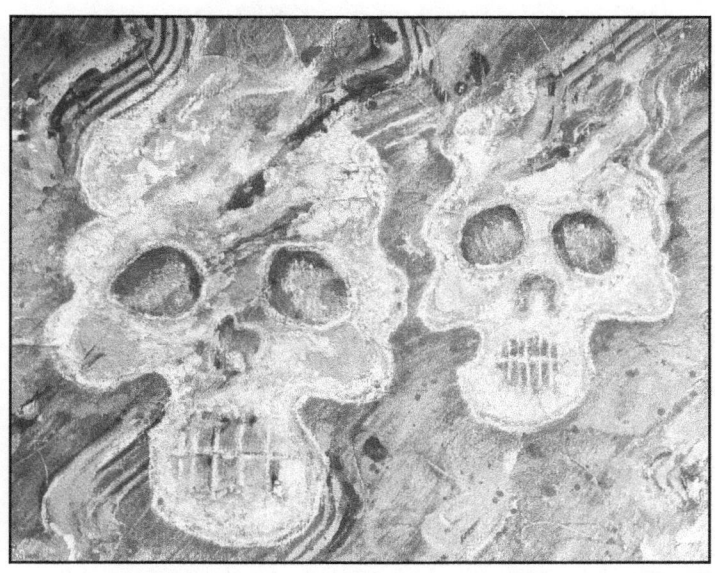

Road Warriors

Determined tires grip the road,
no breaking for nature's speed bumps.
Cheeks stuffed, zigzagging squirrels
never reach the other side,
crumpled by two tons of moving metal,
bloody entrails spread like minced meat.
Diamondback tangled in orange road netting,
mouth stretched open, fixed in a frozen attack.
Another hit and run leaves
a lost cougar limp and lifeless.

Crows pick at flesh and shattered bones
only to become victims to the unyielding chariots,
feathers flapping like a fancy dancer's headdress.
Irrelevant animals crisp to leather along asphalt edges.
No sirens, no lights, no rescue
for the fallen messengers.

Let me scrape up the pieces,
make offerings of cornmeal, tobacco,
and return them to the universe
so they may finish their journey.

Bovines herd through the canyon.
Heavy hooves kick up clouds of dirt and flies,
trampling whatever crosses their path.
No stopping for children zigzagging on bicycles,
leaving the innocent with scrapes and contusions.
Joggers flattened by one ton of Black Angus,
spandex appendages abandoned in the dust.

The homeless swoop in with cardboard signs
picking through pockets and backpacks.
It's not like they're endangered;
it's just another fish with legs.

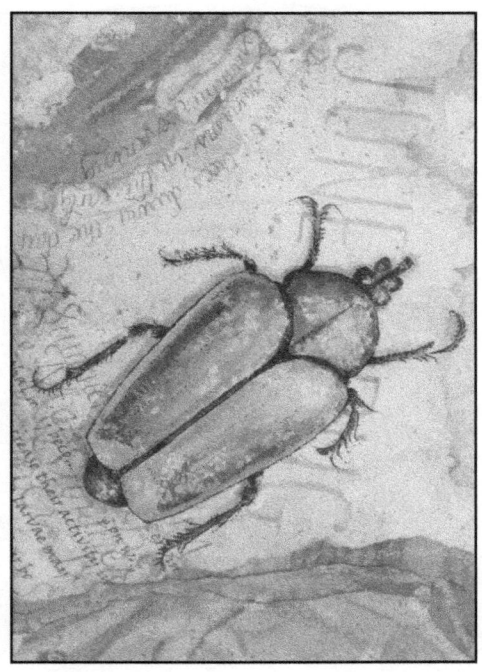

Shaman's Toolbox

Nocturnal victim of russet and ivory
fuses to the asphalt as
cars rush past in a parallel universe.

Sacred tools at my side,
gloves, newspaper and a garden trowel,
I kneel on the blistering gravel.
Squeezing the sun from my eyes,
the fisted talons come into focus.
The carnivorous beak, still.
Eyes fixed in a death stare.

With prayer and intention,
I wrap the fallen raptor
in a shroud of Sunday funnies.
Flesh beetles drop from frayed edges.

Hidden in the safety
of a Steve Madden shoebox,
cornmeal and tobacco
powder the decay,
the beauty, the silence.

A balanced pyramid
of precambrian rocks
holds the spirit deep in the arms
of a dry California hillside.

Beneath the unforgiving
shade of yarrow and sagebrush,
heat blows across my face,
and I wipe the grieving sweat
that stings my eyes.

Interview With Coyote

Abandoned, broken, leaning against a roadside cross.
A new day for Coyote, just another day for me.

Coyote, tell me, did you see it comin'?

Nobody ever sees it comin', my sister.
Too busy watchin' out for the arched neck of my enemy.
Too distracted listenin' for the howls of territorial war.

Was there no escape for you, Old Man?

I did not want the escape, pale sister.
The cracks, the curves, all painted in the blood
of every pack brother that's stood at this cross in the road.
The deafening upheaval came.
The earth split wide enough to swallow all my relatives,
and I surrendered.

Were you afraid, Barking Jackal?

Fur bristled up my back.
My nails chiseled deep
in the hardened-soot-covered field.
My eyes narrowed to slits.
My lungs inhaled the dusty night.
Is that being afraid?

So, this was a humbling experience for you, Brave Brother?

I trembled in awe of its cunning power,
but I was not humbled, sad sister,
to be plucked from the pack,
to thrash from the relentless squeezing of the skins.
To drip warm and weak is an honor.

Any words of wisdom for your cousins, Phantom Wolf?

Only this, weeping sister-
cease to be an obstacle in its path.
The invasion cannot be stopped.
Drop your pelts and dance through the Wall of Fire.
Create the world and hang the stars
before your nose turns black as raven.

Abandoned, broken,
I leaned a plastic tulip against the roadside cross.

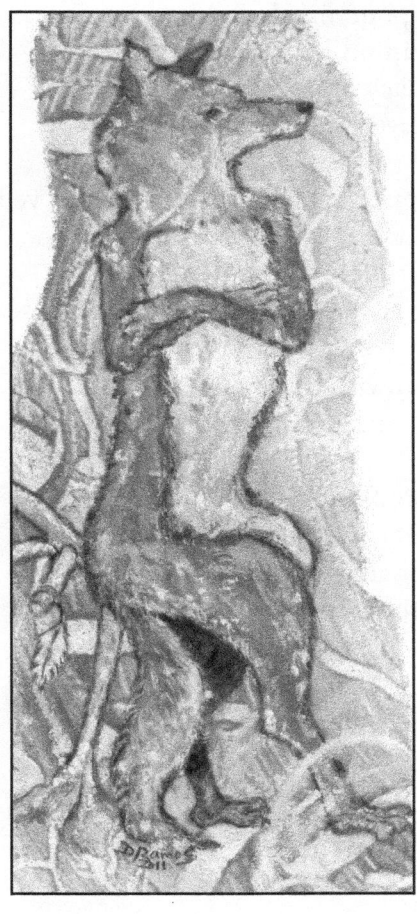

Beneath the Canopy

The Amazon scared me,
but not the greens of ferns and philodendrons,
not the pinks of the shy river dolphins,
not the orange fruit of the dripping sunset.
It was the not knowing.

How would I survive the orchestra
of bubbly fluids in my guts?
The constricted pounding behind my eyes?
Or the monkey mind of an insomniac?
I had the pharmacy of pills in my bag,
and still, I was feverish.

Beneath a canopy of macaw reds and toucan yellows,
anxiety settled in the seat of a canoe
motoring down the river road.
A butterfly with tissue-paper wings
brushed my face and rested
on the walnut brown skin of our guide.
I was becoming a part of the painting.

While we explored leaf-cutter trails,
cleaned yucca roots to make bread,
and sipped the shaman's brew of ayahuasca,
behemoth cockroaches filled
every cranny of our open bags and shoes.
The prehistoric scarabs
will miss my screams the most.

But it was the blue jungle rains
that slowed the pumping of my heart,
and the carbon sink of new air
that quieted the static in my head.
I surrendered to the peace of it,
to the simplicity.
I surrendered until the aging core of my body
fell into the chanting hands of the Amazon.

When Columbus Never Actually Landed in America

What if Columbus just stopped by the Cove of Caobana
for barbadine tea and a lungful of fresh tobacco,
lingering only to enjoy the uncontaminated view
and the All-You-Can-Eat-Roasted-Boar Buffet.

Any decent servant of servants
would politely excuse himself,
return home with gifts of quetzal fans
and carved figurines of
smiling natives, bare and unashamed,
for the fair Queen of Castile.

Suppose bearded strangers,
saddled on steaming horses,
did not come to conquer,
to burn heroes alive,
to feed native babies to hungry war dogs,
but came to trade pelts for pearls,
to play Cuban bingo in silver temples.
And before guests paddle
across shining water in dugout canoes,
jeweled crosses would be laid at the feet of kings
for such indigenous hospitality.

Scattered kingdoms, cupped in paradise,
would be restored, surrounded by
leafy jungles, virgin sand, and turquoise lagoons,
while buried veins of gold squeeze the earth's core
to keep the planet spinning smoothly on her axis.

Imagine that everyone just sent an occasional postcard
and went back home to their
stone castles, icy dwellings, and banana leaf huts,
leaving humanity compatible with land, water, air,
an undisturbed olive soaked in a tropical martini.

When I am Poetry

Tried to meditate
and listen to the question.
Sat with legs crossed,
ass cushioned on pillows,
palms together,
fingertips touching.

My face twitches with
the anxiety of being still.
Inhale the light
cupped in the delicate sacrum.
Exhale droplets of fog.

When I am poetry,
I stop fidgeting.
I am no longer small
in this plump world.
I am written
with perfect line breaks
and balanced stanzas.

The virgin page
releases the wild woman,
arouses the warrior,
and replaces the soul
with a thousand wings.

About the Author

Deborah Ramos, a native of Ocean Beach, San Diego, has been evolving as an artist and writer since high school. She is a graduate of San Diego State University, where she studied art, textiles, costume design and history of theater. Deborah has worked in costume shops, print shops, and flea markets, but art and writing have always been her passion.

Deborah's poems are powerful, sensual and visceral, using language that is full of vision and attitude. Her poetry has appeared in *SageWoman Magazine, League of Laboring Poets, Rattlesnake Press, A Year in Ink Anthology,* and *River of Earth and Sky, Poems for the Twenty-First Century.* Her photography and art can be seen in local art galleries in San Diego. Deborah is a recently retired Special Education Para-professional, having worked with special needs high school students for 20 years.

Now, her creative life includes spending more time traveling, writing, painting, exploring photography, camping in the meadow and enjoying her granddaughters. Her astrological sign is Cancer, and she was born in the year of the Tiger, an interesting combination of forces. Her search for balance continues.

You can visit Deborah at:

redearthspirit@yahoo.com
www.risinggoddessart.blogspot.com